WHEN ROBERT WENT TO STAY

By the same author

WHEN ROBERT WENT TO PLAY GROUP
ROBERT'S PLAYGROUP FRIENDS
ROBERT AND GREAT GRANNY
FRONT PAGE DOG (Hopscotch books)

Anne Rooke

When Robert
Went to Stay

Illustrated by Lesley Smith

HODDER AND STOUGHTON
LONDON SYDNEY AUCKLAND TORONTO

For George

British Library Cataloguing in Publication Data

Rooke, Anne
   When Robert went to stay.
   I. Title   II. Smith, Lesley
   823'.914[J]   PZ7

   ISBN 0-340-40871-5

Text copyright © Anne Rooke 1987
Illustrations copyright © Hodder and Stoughton 1987

First published 1987

Published by Hodder and Stoughton Children's Books,
a division of Hodder and Stoughton Ltd,
Mill Road, Dunton Green, Sevenoaks, Kent TN13 2YJ

Photoset by Rowland Phototypesetting Ltd,
Bury St Edmunds, Suffolk

Printed in Great Britain by T. J. Press (Padstow) Ltd,
Padstow, Cornwall

Contents

Robert Gets a Letter

Robert had never been away to stay all by himself.

He had slept away from home when he had a holiday in a tent, but his mother and father were with him. He had never been away to stay with his own suitcase with only his things in it until, one day, he did. And this is how it happened.

Every year at Christmas time Robert's Great Granny came to stay at Robert's house. She lived in London in a flat all by herself. She was very, very old and couldn't move easily – she had two sticks to walk with – but she had kind neighbours who kept an eye on her. So she was able to carry on living all by herself. But nobody ever came to stay with Great Granny. They couldn't, because she only had one bed and she slept in that.

When Robert went to see her with his mother and father and little sister Susan they just stayed for tea and then went away.

'Do you have to go so soon?' Great Granny

asked. 'You've only just come.'

'You must come and stay with us soon,' Robert's mother said. 'I don't like to think of you here all by yourself.'

In the car on the way home Robert said, 'I don't like to think of Great Granny there all by herself.'

'Don't you, dear?' said his mother, reaching over to wipe Susan's runny nose.

'No,' said Robert. 'I don't.'

The very next Sunday morning Robert's father telephoned Great Granny to see how she was getting on.

'Can I speak to her – please?' Robert asked.

His father nodded. 'Make it snappy,' he whispered.

'Hullo, Great Granny,' Robert said in a loud voice. 'I'll come and stay with you.'

'Oh?' said Great Granny in a surprised voice.

'It's my last day at play group soon,' Robert went on, 'and then I'll come and stay. All right?'

'Oh,' said Great Granny again, as Robert handed the telephone receiver back to his father. 'Well, fancy that,' she said.

'Don't worry, Gran,' said Robert's father. 'He's full of crackpot notions.'

A few days later Robert got a real letter through the post. He couldn't remember having one of

those before, and this is what it said:

Dear Robert,
    I would love you to come and stay if you really want to. Mrs Hargreaves will lend me her camp-bed and look after us if we run into trouble. Ask your mother and father to telephone me and we will see what we can arrange.

With all my love,
Great Granny

Robert's mother read it all out to him.
    Robert smiled and laughed and jumped about a bit, but his mother looked thoughtful.

'It's an awful lot for Great Granny at her age,' she said. 'It's no joke looking after a four-year-old.'

'I'm nearly five,' said Robert. 'I'll look after *her*. That's what I'll do.'

'Mmmm,' said his mother. 'Well, we'll see.'

When Robert's father saw the letter he said, 'Lucky Rob. I wouldn't mind a few days of Gran's cooking. I used to love staying with her.'

'Yes, but she was twenty years younger then,' said Robert's mother. 'She's ninety now. She's far too old to look after a child.'

'Don't you believe it,' said Robert's father. 'She and Mrs Hargreaves will love it. And it'll give you a bit of a break. I should let him go.'

'Well,' said Robert's mother, 'I can always fetch him back if it doesn't work out.'

'It will work out,' said Robert to Susan who was curling her hair round a Stickle Brick. 'It's not a crackpot notion. It's a *good idea*.'

'Good idea,' Susan nearly said and then she began to yell because the Stickle Brick got stuck in her hair.

Robert's father bent down to try to untangle the spiky brick. 'Then I'll telephone Gran tonight. Be still, Susan. And we'll fix up a visit.'

Treasure and Custard

Robert heard his father on the telephone to Great Granny while Susan was having her bath that evening. 'All right, Gran,' Robert's father said. 'Wednesday week it is, then. Early afternoon. He's certainly looking forward to it. We are too.'

Robert went upstairs and pulled out a red suitcase from under his parents' bed. He carried and pushed it along to his bedroom and tried to open the catches. He pushed and pushed at the round knobs with a keyhole in the middle. Suddenly one catch flew open and hit his hand hard. Robert opened his mouth to yell and then shut it again. Instead, he flapped his hand about to take the pain away and set about the other catch. That flew open too and he pushed open the lid and looked at the shiny satin lining with bunched-up pockets at the back. He pushed his hand into one of the pockets and felt something hard and round. This time he did let out a yell. It was a dark gold coin.

Robert ran through to his mother in the bath-room. 'Look,' he shouted. 'I've found treasure. Real gold treasure.'

'What?' said his mother, lifting Susan out of the bath. She looked at the coin in Robert's hand. 'It's a pound coin,' she said. 'Where did you find that?'

'In your suitcase,' said Robert. 'I'm packing,' he explained.

'Well, leave it on the shelf here,' said his mother. 'I'll put it in my purse later.'

Robert went back to the suitcase and stuck his hands in the pockets again. But there was no more treasure. He sighed and got on with his packing.

He put his slippers that looked like foxes into the suitcase. Next he found Panda and his model dinosaurs and put those in. He felt under his pillow and pulled out a little old eiderdown. He liked to hold the corner of it when he went to sleep. He had had it since he was a baby and it looked rather ragged now, so his father called it 'Robert's Horror'. He put that on top of the dinosaurs and then ran downstairs to a cupboard in the dining room.

There he found the photograph albums. He looked through one until he came to a photo of his parents, Susan and him at Christmas time. Great Granny had taken it for them and the top of

his father's head wasn't in the picture – only his mouth and nose. Robert took it carefully out of the album, ran back upstairs and put the photograph in the suitcase.

'I've done my packing,' he shouted to his mother as she came out of the bathroom carrying Susan.

She came into his bedroom. 'I've had an idea,' she said.

'Good,' said Robert.

'I thought you could keep that treasure you found,' she said, sitting down on Robert's bed. 'And, if you were feeling very kind, you might use it to take Great Granny to a coffee shop. How about that?'

'Yes, yes,' shouted Robert giving his mother and Susan a hug. 'And I'll get you a present. And one for Dad. And one for Susan – perhaps.'

'Well,' said his mother standing up again. 'I think you'll have to ask Daddy for more treasure if you're to do all that.'

Suddenly Robert's father appeared in the doorway. 'Treasure?' he said. 'You'll have to help me dig the garden tomorrow, Robert. That's the best way to look for treasure.'

'Yes, I'll do that,' said Robert. 'I like finding treasure.'

Later that evening when Susan was in bed Robert found his father lighting the fire in the sitting room.

'Did you go away to stay when you were my age?' Robert asked.

'Yes, I expect so,' said his father piling coal on to the flame.

'What's it like?' Robert asked.

His father sat back on his heels to watch the fire. 'Well, I liked it,' he said, 'but I just went to the house next door, you see. The people there were called Mr and Mrs Ware and they looked after me sometimes if my parents went away or had a night out.'

'What was the best thing?' Robert asked.

'Having a cup of custard at bed-time,' said his father at once. 'Mrs Ware knew I loved custard and she always made it for me. And the first night I stayed with them by myself she helped me climb up into their spare bed from a blue wicker chair and then she gave me a cup of custard to keep me happy. And when I woke up in the morning I'd fallen out of bed.'

'Why?' Robert asked.

'I didn't do it on purpose,' his father said, pushing in the metal flap at the bottom of the grate. 'It just happened. I suppose I was used to a cot with sides to keep me in. It didn't matter anyway. The bedclothes came down with me and kept me warm. Mr Ware said I could sleep on the floor next time and save myself the trouble of falling out.'

'Did you?' asked Robert.

'No,' said his father. 'But Mrs Ware tucked the bedclothes in so tight I could scarcely move – let alone fall out.'

'Did you take a suitcase?' Robert asked.

'No. I just carried my pyjamas around to their house. And I took my toy monkey, called Jacko. He sat beside me to watch their television. We didn't have a television at home – not many people did then. We used to watch Sooty, I remember.'

'I watch Sooty too,' said Robert.

'Yes. Sooty must be getting quite old – like me,' said his father picking up the log basket to go and fill it from the pile by the back door. 'Isn't it time you went to bed? The more time you spend asleep the sooner your visit to Great Granny will come.'

So Robert went to bed as quickly as he could that evening. But he didn't go to sleep as quickly. He kept thinking and wondering about staying at Great Granny's and what custard might feel like drunk out of a cup.

The Journey

At last the day came for Robert to go to Great Granny's.

His mother had bought him some new pyjamas because his old ones had got very small and the top part wouldn't meet the trousers any more. His new pyjamas had red, orange, green, yellow and blue stripes on the top half, and blue trousers. Robert didn't wear them at all but put them straight into the red suitcase and carried on wearing his old ones.

His mother also packed two tee-shirts, a proper shirt, a spare jumper, and pants, vests and socks. Robert tried packing his father's red spotted handkerchief but his mother took it out and put it back in his father's drawer. So Robert had to take two handkerchiefs with He Man on them instead.

Lastly his mother packed a drawing book and some felt pens, four picture books and a real story book for bed-time. But, when she packed

Robert's toothbrush and flannel in a plastic bag into the pocket at the back of the suitcase, she found the photograph of the family at Christmas.

'What on earth is this doing here?' she asked Robert, getting it out to look at it.

'It's so that I don't forget what you look like,' Robert explained.

His mother began to laugh as she looked at the photo.

'Oh well,' she said. 'It will give Great Granny a good laugh.' And she stuffed it back into the suitcase pocket.

'Now, is there anything else you need?' she said, looking hard at the things in the suitcase.

'Can I take those yoghurts in the fridge?' Robert asked.

'No,' said his mother.

'Then Susan will eat them all,' said Robert.

'Yes,' said his mother. 'But you'll have one for lunch – a very early lunch – because we have to catch something. Guess what?'

Robert frowned and shook his head. He didn't want to guess wrong.

'A train,' said his mother.

Robert *was* pleased. He'd always thought his mother would take him to Great Granny's in the car as usual. But no, they were to go by train. Susan was going to spend the afternoon with her friend Daisy next door and Robert and his mother were going on the train to London.

'You'll be five next month,' his mother said, 'and then I'll have to pay for you. This is your last chance to go free. So I thought we'd better take it.'

Robert nodded happily. And then he had another thought. 'Will we go on the Underground?' he asked.

'That's right,' said his mother. 'Perhaps we'd better pack your dressing gown.'

'It's too small,' said Robert.

'Never mind,' said his mother.

And Robert said nothing because he was too busy thinking about the train journey.

Robert had been on a train with his Uncle Frank and the other children in his play group. But that had only been a short journey, and the journey to London went on for a long time. It went on for such a long time that Robert began to wonder if it would ever end. He wanted to get out at every station in case it was London. So his mother said it wouldn't be long and he'd know when to get off because everybody else would too. And at last he saw the great, wide, shiny, grey River Thames. The train went over a bridge and there they were at the London station.

There were such a lot of people on the station

trying to give their tickets to the ticket collector
that Robert got quite frightened in case he lost
his mother. He hung on to her coat while she
searched for her ticket in her bag and tried to
keep the red suitcase from getting kicked. Then
he held her hand tightly while she gave in her
ticket and they walked to the top of the stairs
going down to the Underground station.

And then Robert went on something he had

never been on before – an escalator. He had to be lifted on by his mother while a kind man behind them lifted on the red suitcase. For a little way the escalator went along straight and then it moved downwards and made itself into stairs. Robert's mother made sure he was standing safely on a step with his hands on the black moving handrail. Robert stood very carefully and watched the people coming up on the other side. Some people smiled at him but he didn't smile back because he'd found that the black handrail didn't move quite fast enough and he kept having to jump his hands a little so that they didn't get left behind.

Suddenly Robert's mother lifted him up as the escalator went flat again at the bottom and she stepped off holding him.

'Did you like that?' she asked as she took Robert's suitcase from the helpful man.

'I think so,' said Robert, getting hold of her hand again. 'Where's the train?'

'Through that arch,' said his mother. 'And hurry. I can hear it coming.'

Robert and his mother went through the arch and Robert's hair stood straight up in a great wind. 'It's the train pushing the air down the tunnel in front of it that does that,' his mother shouted above the noise of the train.

'It smells funny,' Robert shouted back.

There were lots of people getting off the train. They did it very fast and the people getting on were very quick too so that there were no empty seats for Robert and his mother when the train lurched off on its way again.

'You hold on to me and I'll hold on to this strap,' his mother said.

So Robert hung on hard as the train went faster and faster, swaying round bends and braking sometimes. Then he saw a woman smiling at him and patting the corner of a seat between her and a little girl.

'Sit down there,' his mother said, but Robert felt shy and looked away from the smiling woman, pretending not to hear. And just then the train braked hard before the next station and Robert fell over flat on to the floor.

His mother picked him up and plonked him down beside the smiling woman, who wasn't smiling any more but saying, 'Oh dear, oh dear,' in a worried way, bending forward to see if Robert's knees were all right. Robert put his hands over his knees and stared out of the window opposite, trying not to cry. Then he felt in his duffle coat pocket and found a handkerchief.

'That's a surprise,' said his mother in a laughing voice.

Robert nodded and blew his nose and began to enjoy the journey again.

So it wasn't early afternoon when Robert and his mother arrived at Great Granny's flat. It was middle-to-late afternoon.

'Oh my word, isn't this fun,' said Great Granny as she opened the door of her flat for them to go in. 'I *have* been looking forward to this. Stay for a cup of tea, dear,' she said to Robert's mother.

'D'you mind if I don't?' asked Robert's mother. 'There's an exhibition of paintings I want to see and I don't know when I'll get another chance.'

'Of course, of course. Yes, run along,' said Great Granny. 'Robert and I will cope, won't we Robert?'

'Goodbye then, Lovey,' said his mother giving Robert a kiss. 'Be good. And I'll telephone tomorrow night.'

Robert nodded.

His mother looked at Great Granny.

'I'll be off then,' she said.

Great Granny put both her sticks under one elbow and held Robert's hand. 'Now don't you worry one bit,' she said to Robert's mother. 'The whole building has been waiting for this visit. It will make our Easter. It really will.'

'Thank you, Gran,' said Robert's mother giving her a kiss and she winked at Robert and went out shutting the door gently behind her.

Tea Together

Robert looked up at Great Granny and saw that she was smiling at him. 'I think it's tea-time,' she said. And still holding Robert's hand she walked very slowly across the sitting room and into her little kitchen.

'I'll do it. I will,' said Robert, running across to the cupboard where Great Granny kept her teacups. He fetched down a yellow cup and saucer and a big white mug with a red dragon on it. 'Can I use this, please?' he asked.

'You may,' said Great Granny plugging in her shiny electric kettle. 'And if you look in that tin you might find something.'

Robert lifted the tin with pictures of castles on it and it felt very heavy. He held it against his chest as he pulled off the lid. Out came a lovely syrupy smell. 'Flapjacks!' he yelled. 'Thank you, Great Granny.'

'Any time,' said Great Granny. 'Provided you let me know you're coming.'

'How many can I have?' Robert asked.

'As many as you like,' said Great Granny. 'Well, within reason,' she added.

'Is three within reason?' asked Robert.

'Yes, but just put out one for me. My teeth aren't as strong as they used to be. And let's be grand and have them on a plate.'

'All right,' said Robert cheerfully, fetching a plate from the cupboard and putting it on the kitchen table.

'Now, a bottle of milk from the fridge, if you please, and we're all set,' said Great Granny. 'Do you like a cup of tea?'

'I like just milk better,' said Robert.

'Then you pour yourself some into the dragon mug. D'you know how to open the bottle?'

Robert nodded because he did know how, but he had never been allowed to do it all by himself. Very carefully he pushed down the middle of the silver top into the bottle and then lifted off the top *without spilling a drop*. He poured some milk into the dragon mug and didn't spill much then either. So Great Granny said, 'Oh well done, dear. And can you pour a drop into my teacup? I'd better pour this hot tea, though – we don't want you getting burnt.'

Then Great Granny sat down very slowly on her kitchen chair and sighed happily. Robert got the kitchen stool, which was a small stepladder as well, and put it next to the table and climbed up to sit on it.

While they drank their tea and milk and ate the flapjacks Robert looked around the kitchen at all Great Granny's things, and Great Granny looked at him. Sometimes they looked at each other and smiled. But they didn't talk much at all.

'There,' said Great Granny, when she had finished her second cup of tea. 'That's better. Let's just put the cups and plates on the draining board. We can wash up after supper. And what do you like to do in the evening?'

'I like watching television,' said Robert.

'Well now, and so do I,' said Great Granny. 'Let's do it together.'

Great Granny stood up slowly and Robert handed her the two walking sticks. 'I'll turn on the television,' he said, and ran into the sitting room.

Now normally Great Granny sat in a special armchair by the window. But today she sat down on a settee opposite the television and Robert sat down beside her. He wriggled backwards until he was right up against the back of the settee with his legs stuck out straight.

Together they watched Laurel and Hardy in a funny cartoon. Robert leant his head against Great Granny's arm and felt it shake when she laughed. The next programme was a serial about

children in the London Docks. Great Granny
hadn't seen the first part and nor had Robert but
she didn't get up to turn it off because Robert had
shut his eyes.

A few minutes later Great Granny saw that his
mouth was a little bit open. Robert had gone
sound asleep. Robert slept and slept all through
the cartoons and right up to the six o'clock news.
Then he woke up with a jump.

'Is it bed-time yet?' he asked in a loud voice.

'Not yet,' said Great Granny. 'But it is nearly

supper-time. What would you like?'

'Have you got any baked beans?' Robert asked.

'Six tins,' said Great Granny, laughing. 'Mrs Hargreaves said that's what you'd want, so she has got me in a good supply. I think I'll have some too.'

'Yes,' said Robert. 'They're very, very good for us.'

'Should we have all six then?' Great Granny asked.

'No, no,' Robert laughed. 'One between us, that's enough.'

'Right you are,' said Great Granny. 'You're the bean expert around here.'

The First Evening

After supper Robert helped Great Granny do the washing-up. He sometimes helped his mother at home, of course, but he always *dried up*. Great Granny let him *wash up*.

She tied a green check apron around his middle and let him kneel on the kitchen stool to reach the things in the sink. He used a white floppy string mop on a stick to rub the plates and spoons and forks. He gave the dragon mug a very careful wipe and Great Granny dried it and left it on the kitchen table so that he could use it whenever he wished.

Then they heard a tap at the door and Mrs Hargreaves came in, using her own key.

'Hullo, Robert,' she said. 'Is everything all right? Is your bed all right? Here's another bottle of milk in case you run out. What a lovely day it's been after yesterday.'

'I haven't seen my bed,' said Robert. 'Where is it? Hullo, Mrs Hargreaves,' he added.

'In the bedroom of course,' said Great Granny.

Robert ran and opened the bedroom door. He saw Great Granny's high bed with a handle hanging over it to help her pull herself up. And low down on the floor beside it he saw a camp-bed with a white sheet turned back over yellow blankets and a sleeping bag folded at the end.

Now, on Robert's bed at home he had a duvet. It was like a great big floppy eiderdown and it saved his mother making a bed with two sheets and blankets every morning. So he was very pleased to see he had a beautiful, white, turned-back sheet and real woolly blankets. And, best of all, the sheet had a white R embroidered in the middle of the turned-back bit.

'It's got a R for Robert on it,' he shouted through to Great Granny and Mrs Hargreaves in the kitchen.

Mrs Hargreaves came into the bedroom. 'Your Great Granny thinks that sheet must be over eighty years old. It really is beautifully embroidered,' she said.

At the head of the camp-bed there was a small red stool instead of a table. 'Little Clio from the flat upstairs has lent you that,' Mrs Hargreaves explained. 'She's longing to meet you. You're about the same age.'

'I've got to look after Great Granny,' Robert said. 'I mightn't have time to meet her.'

'Well, you're sure to see her going in and out. I
saw her on the landing near the lift just now.'
And Mrs Hargreaves went back to talk to Great
Granny.

Robert carried and pulled his suitcase from the
front door into the bedroom. He flopped it down
on its side and undid the catches. Very quickly he
pulled off his clothes and rummaged in the suitcase for his new pyjamas. He found them and
pulled them out of their see-through packet and
put them on. Then he ran to show Great Granny.

'Look at my new pyjamas, Great Granny,' he
shouted.

'Good heavens, what stripes,' said Great

Granny. 'I have *never* seen such gorgeous pyjamas. What a shame you can't wear them to the
park.'

Mrs Hargreaves laughed. 'I'll be off,' she said.
'Just knock on the wall if you need anything.
And I'll pop in some time after breakfast. Have
you got everything you need for breakfast?'

'Yes, thank you,' said Great Granny.

'Goodbye. See you tomorrow,' said Robert.

'Sleep well, dear,' said Mrs Hargreaves and
went back to her flat next door.

'Now,' said Great Granny, 'it's bath-time and
I dare say you've folded your clothes nicely.'

Robert shot back into the bedroom and pulled
his vest and tee-shirt out of his jumper. He folded
his trousers and looked around for his socks.
One was under Great Granny's bed. The other
one had disappeared. 'Do you know where my
other sock is?' he called to Great Granny.

'On your foot?' Great Granny called back.

'No. Susan must have taken it,' he said. 'Oh,
no,' he added as he remembered Susan wasn't
there.

'It'll turn up,' said Great Granny, 'I'll run your
bath. Have you got a toothbrush?'

'Yes, and a flannel,' said Robert, pulling them
out of the pocket at the back of the suitcase. At
the same time he found the photograph of his
family and propped it up on Great Granny's

bedside table next to the one of his Great Grandfather.

'I'm coming,' he called and ran through into
the steamy bathroom.

When the bath was full enough Great Granny
turned off the taps and Robert climbed in. It was
a pale pink bath and felt different from the white
one at home. The soap was different too. He
picked it up.

'It's transparent. That means you can see
through it,' Great Granny explained. 'But it
works just like ordinary soap.'

Robert rubbed a bit on his knees and one
shoulder.

'Come on now,' said Great Granny, 'A good
soaping all over.'

'Not in my eyes, though,' said Robert.

'No, not in your eyes, old Clever Boots,'
Great Granny said. 'What happened to your
knees?'

'I fell over on the Underground train,' Robert explained. 'I had to sit next to a lady with a funny voice – and a girl.'

Great Granny nodded. 'They'll be better in a day or two.'

'Can I have a story – please?' Robert asked.

'At this late hour?' said Great Granny. 'When I was your age I had been in bed for *hours* by now.'

'What time did you go to bed?' Robert asked. 'I go at half past six.'

'Well,' said Great Granny. 'It is now half past *seven*. So out of that bath and into that bed.'

A few minutes later Robert was tucked up under the beautifully embroidered sheet on Mrs Hargreaves's camp-bed.

'I've said a prayer for you instead of Susan tonight,' he told Great Granny.

'Thank you,' said Great Granny. 'I'll say one for Susan instead. And I'm very sorry but I can't bend over to kiss you good night.'

Quick as a flash Robert jumped up and climbed on to Great Granny's high bed, pulling himself up by the useful hanging handle. 'Now you can,' he said.

So Great Granny did. 'Good night. Sleep tight. Wake up bright in the morning light. And not before,' she said.

Robert got back into bed and Great Granny went out, leaving the door into the sitting room open a crack. Robert didn't go to sleep for quite a long time. He felt very strange in his new pyjamas and white sheets. But when Great Granny came to bed later on she saw that he was fast asleep with a corner of his old eider down Horror clutched in his hand.

Kangaroos and Elephants

Next morning Robert woke up very early. He sat up and saw that Great Granny was still asleep in her high bed beside him. His mother had told him to make sure Great Granny had a rest every afternoon and that he mustn't tire her out, so he lay down again and looked at the wallpaper and the bit of sky he could see where the curtains didn't quite meet.

Suddenly, 'Good morning,' said Great Granny, feeling for her glasses on her bedside table. 'Did you sleep well?'

'I've been awake for ages,' said Robert, sitting up.

'You're very low down there,' said Great Granny. 'Not like me when I went to stay with *my* Granny. I had an enormous bed.'

'Were you very big?' Robert asked.

'Oh, no,' said Great Granny. 'I was about your size. I was four and three-quarters.'

'So am I. That's nearly five,' said Robert. 'Did

you sleep at your Granny's?'

'I did indeed. *And* I had a rest in the afternoon. And, do you know, *she* lived in London too. Just as I do now. But she lived in a great big house with lots of bedrooms.'

'Why?' Robert asked.

'I can't think why,' said Great Granny. 'There was only Granny and Jane who looked after her and a young girl who dusted and swept.'

'Like Cinderella?' asked Robert.

'No, not like Cinderella,' said Great Granny. 'She didn't wear rags and she seemed very happy. And I'm sure she never went off to a ball in a pumpkin. She was called Margaret and I liked her very much.

'I remember the first time I went to stay with Granny all by myself, I went on the train.'

'Like me,' Robert shouted.

'Ah, but in those days we had a real puffing engine to pull the train. My father took me to say thank you to the engine driver when we got to London and I *did* get a surprise. The driver's face was all black with soot from the engine's fire and his eyes were red-rimmed from the heat. But he'd got to London dead on time, so he was very pleased. My father began to talk to him but suddenly we were deafened by an engine letting off steam near us. It was a terrible noise. A sort of whistling shriek and steam shot up in the air and

swirled down over the platform. My word, it did make me jump, and I was just about to cry when my father lifted me up and let me give his newspaper to the kind engine driver. And then he carried me and my suitcase and my doll out of the station and we took a cab to Granny's house.'

'Is that like the Underground?' Robert asked.

'No – not at all. A cab was a shiny black carriage pulled by a horse. Even the buses were pulled by horses in those days. I really wanted to go on a bus and sit up on top to see the sights – but my father said a cab would be quicker.

'Well, we soon arrived at Granny's house and

she came running out of her front door to give us a hug. You see she was *much* younger then than I am now and she could skip and hop quite easily.'

'Like a kangaroo?' Robert asked.

Great Granny thought. 'More like a rabbit, really. A kangaroo could jump right across this bedroom and my Granny couldn't do that.'

Robert laughed and Great Granny laughed too. 'But, thinking of kangaroos,' she went on, 'that's reminded me of a splendid treat she gave me.'

'I like treats,' said Robert.

'Me too,' Great Granny agreed. 'And so did my Granny. Because the next day, when I was having breakfast with her – porridge and eggs and bacon *always* – she said "Rose, my dear, let's go to the Zoo. I haven't been for ages and I badly need a ride on an elephant."'

'I've *never* had a ride on an elephant,' said Robert.

'No, nor had I,' said Great Granny. 'So you can imagine how excited I was. And after breakfast we went straight off to the Zoo.'

'In a cab?' Robert asked.

'No, we walked,' said Great Granny. 'Granny liked walking – very briskly – so I had to trot. My legs were shorter than yours even.'

'Mine are very long,' said Robert.

'So I was a bit puffed when we got to the Zoo.

But I soon forgot to be tired. I saw camels and bears, and monkeys who threw their fruit at the visitors and generally behaved very badly. There was a house full of the most dreadfully noisy parrots too. In fact they were making such a noise Granny took me out because I began to cry. We went into the lion house and that smelt so much I held my nose, but Granny said that was not at all polite to the lions. So I let go of my nose because I didn't want to be rude to a lion, did I?'

'No, or he might have gobbled you up,' said Robert. 'Did you go on the elephant next?'

'Not straight away,' said Great Granny. 'I remember Granny sitting on a bench while I had a ride on a camel. But it was not a polite camel and it kept spitting at its keeper until it was taken back to the camel house in disgrace. Granny said it served it right.'

Robert nodded. 'I think so too,' he said.

'And then, at last, the elephant was brought out,' said Great Granny. 'And I had never seen anything so *enormous* in all my life.'

'Was it an African elephant or an Indian elephant?' Robert asked.

'An Indian one, I should think,' said Great Granny. 'And there was a special flight of stairs to climb up to get to the chair on his back.'

'Like getting on an aeroplane,' Robert suggested.

'Exactly,' said Great Granny, very pleased. 'And when we were up there it felt almost like being in an aeroplane – we were so high. And we swayed along as the elephant, very gently and carefully, walked down the flowery paths past all the other animals. I enjoyed it so much I never wanted it to stop. And Granny said she felt the same and that we'd have to go and have a ride on the elephant *every* time I came to London.'

'Did you?' Robert asked.

'I think I did,' said Great Granny. 'And when I was a young woman I can remember my last

visit with Granny to the Zoo. She was getting rather stiff by then – and so was the elephant, I expect – but the keepers helped her up the steps on to the long chair and, as we walked along, the elephant plucked an orange marigold flower in his trunk. Then he swung his trunk up behind him and waved the flower in front of Granny. So she took it and put it in her buttonhole and said, "Thank you kindly, dear sir." She was always most polite.'

Robert said 'Can *we* go to the Zoo, Great Granny, please?'

'Well, I really am too old for such a trip by myself with you,' said Great Granny sadly. And then her voice cheered up and she said, 'But what about your birthday treat? That's coming up soon, isn't it?'

Robert nodded.

'Then I'll tell you what,' said Great Granny. 'I'll ask your father to bring you back to London one day and we can all go to the Zoo together. How about that?'

'Yes – yes – yes,' shouted Robert. 'And I'll go on the elephant.'

'And the camel,' said Great Granny.

'Well –' said Robert.

'Yes, well –' laughed Great Granny. 'We'll have to see about that. And now I think we'd better get up, don't you?'

Porridge

Great Granny pushed back the bedclothes and held on to the handle above her bed, carefully swinging her legs to the ground.

'That's clever,' said Robert.

'I think so too,' whispered Great Granny. 'Now,' she said as she pulled on her dressing gown. 'Shall we wash and dress before breakfast or afterwards? What do you do at home?'

Robert thought. 'I get dressed first at home,' he said. 'So can we have breakfast in our dressing gowns instead? My dressing gown's a bit small. But Mummy said it would do.'

'Fine,' said Great Granny. 'Then you get the cups and bowls out while I go to the bathroom.'

Robert looked in all the kitchen cupboards and in the small fridge and got out a yellow cup and saucer, two bowls, two spoons, a bottle of milk and a jar of marmalade.

'That's the way,' said Great Granny as she came into the kitchen. 'But I'm feeling like the

Three Bears this morning. Can you guess what I want to eat?'

'Goldilocks?' Robert asked.

'Goldilocks would taste very nasty indeed. No, I want . . .'

'PORRIDGE,' shouted Robert.

'Exactly,' said Great Granny. 'If you look in that cupboard you'll find a red packet of porridge oats.'

Robert found the packet.

'And if you fill up your dragon mug with oats that will be enough. Good. Now, tip them into this saucepan.'

'Now what?' Robert asked when he had done that.

'Fill up the mug with water from the tap. But turn the tap on slowly – we don't want a shower-bath.'

'Shall I pour it on the oats?' Robert asked.

Great Granny passed him a wooden spoon. 'Yes,' she said. 'And then pour on a full mug of milk. I'll put in a pinch of salt and you stir carefully. Lovely.'

Great Granny turned on her electric stove and put the saucepan on to a hot plate. She leant on one of her sticks and stirred the porridge as it cooked.

'I don't like porridge,' said Robert.

'Oh,' said Great Granny. She stirred for a bit

longer and then pulled the saucepan off the hot plate. 'I don't like it too hot or too cold or too lumpy either. I like it just right with a little milk and sugar. But of course – I remember – ' she went on. 'Your great grandfather – who was also called Robert, you know – he liked it the Scottish way. I suppose that's how you like it too, isn't it?'

'I'm not sure,' said Robert.

'Oh, I expect it is,' said Great Granny. 'No sticky sugar for you Roberts. Just a bit of extra salt and you stand up to eat it. I'll pour a bit on to a saucer for you so that it can spread out and cool, and not keep you standing about too long.'

So Great Granny poured a very little bit of the porridge on to a yellow saucer and sprinkled it

with salt. 'And if you like you can walk up and
down while you eat it,' she said.

Robert took a spoon and the saucer and
walked across the kitchen from the fridge to the
door while he ate it. Great Granny had given him
so little porridge that he had finished it in two
turns.

'Perhaps you ought to have some more,' Great
Granny suggested. 'It looks a windy day outside
and we'll need to eat a good breakfast.'

'Yes,' said Robert. 'And can I have some sugar
on it this time – *and* walk up and down again?'

'Well,' said Great Granny, 'I don't know what
your Great Grandfather would have said, do
you?'

'No,' said Robert.

'Oh yes, I do though,' said Great Granny, laughing. 'He'd have said, "Get on and eat it – it's sticking to the saucepan."'

Then she poured some more on to Robert's saucer and the rest into a bowl for herself. 'Just look at the time,' she said, glancing at the kitchen clock. 'Can you turn on the top knob on the radio, Robert? I always like to hear the news.'

So Great Granny sat down comfortably to eat her porridge and Robert walked up and down again with his, being careful not to walk on the lines between the kitchen floor tiles.

'Susan likes porridge even when she's sitting down,' Robert said when Great Granny turned off the radio.

'Thank heavens for that,' said Great Granny.

'She might fall over if she walked about with it,' said Robert.

'Sure to,' Great Granny agreed. 'She and I are much safer sitting down.'

'But I still don't like porridge *very* much,' Robert said, putting down the empty saucer.

'Oh well,' said Great Granny, 'I'm sure you will when you're ninety.'

Great Granny's Treat

Great Granny and Robert did the breakfast washing-up, got dressed and tidied the flat.

'What shall we do this morning?' Great Granny asked as she put her small vacuum cleaner away in the kitchen cupboard.

'Can we go shopping?' Robert asked.

'Well, kind Mrs Hargreaves got me in a bit of food yesterday. I don't think there's anything we need just yet,' Great Granny replied.

'Then why don't *we* do *her* shopping?' Robert suggested. 'Then we'll be kind too.'

'All right,' said Great Granny. 'Put your coat on and we'll go down to the shops.'

Great Granny put on her winter coat and hat and hung her bag around her neck. Robert fetched her two long metal outdoor walking sticks from their place by the front door.

'Ready?' Great Granny asked. 'On your marks, get set, GO,' she said and she stepped out of her front door and let Robert lock it behind them.

Robert ran ahead and rang Mrs Hargreaves's front door bell.

'Hullo, Robert,' said Mrs Hargreaves when she opened the door. 'Where are you going?'

'We're going to do your shopping,' Robert told her.

Mrs Hargreaves looked across at Great Granny.

'I'm sure there's something you want,' said Great Granny. 'And we're going out anyway.'

Mrs Hargreaves thought hard. 'I'm clean out of bicarbonate of soda. Could you get me some, Robert?'

Robert looked back at Great Granny. 'I can't remember that,' he said.

'Then I'll remind you,' Great Granny promised. 'Goodbye,' she said to Mrs Hargreaves.

'Go carefully, both of you,' said Mrs Hargreaves.

'We will,' said Great Granny, getting into the lift. Robert followed her and pressed the button to make the lift go down.

'Now,' said Great Granny when they reached the pavement outside the flats, 'What is it we've got to get?'

'Something of soda,' said Robert.

'Bicarbonate of soda. I knew you'd remember,' said Great Granny. 'Left turn and straight ahead.'

Luckily there was a small supermarket not far down the road. Robert had expected the shops in London to be bigger than the ones in his village at home, but this supermarket only had space for one alley-way down and back. 'I'm very glad it's small,' Great Granny said. 'It saves me a lot of walking.' And she picked up a wire basket. 'Now, it'll be near the flour and sugar I expect. Let's get looking.'

So Robert went past the fruit and vegetables and butter and cheese. He looked along the shelves of bread and biscuits and heard Great Granny say, 'Ah, yeast. I'll need a packet of

that.' Then she said, 'You're getting very warm indeed, Robert. No, don't go too far. Back a bit and down a bit. D'you see? Those little round white drums with black writing.'

Robert saw several different types of round box. 'I can't read what they say,' he said.

'Never mind,' Great Granny said. 'I can. Hold them up and I'll have a look.'

Robert held up two drums. 'That's cream of tartar,' said Great Granny, 'but this is it. Bicarbonate of soda. Well done. Pop it in my basket.'

'What's it for?' Robert asked as they went slowly to the check-out counter to pay.

'Bee stings and baking,' said Great Granny. 'Have you ever been stung by a bee?'

'No,' said Robert.

'Lucky boy,' said Great Granny. 'I have, when I was even younger than you.'

'Can you tell me about it?' Robert asked.

'Later,' said Great Granny paying for the bicarbonate of soda and yeast and handing the box to Robert. 'Can you put this in your duffle coat pocket?' she asked. 'It isn't very big.'

Robert pushed the box into his pocket and his fingers touched something hard. He jumped a little and grabbed Great Granny's hand as he pulled a pound coin out of his pocket.

'Mummy gave me this,' he shouted, 'for us to go to a coffee shop.'

Great Granny stopped in the door of the shop.

'Excuse me, Madam,' said a man carrying a huge tray of loaves of bread and buns. 'May I come by?'

'Oh, I am sorry,' said Great Granny, stepping out on to the pavement. 'But I've just been told of a splendid treat.'

'I'm taking Great Granny to a coffee shop,' Robert told the man.

'That's a great idea,' said the man going into the shop. 'Enjoy yourselves.'

'We shall,' said Great Granny. And she turned to Robert and said, 'Shall we go to that new hamburger place that's opened down the road? I've been longing to see inside it.'

Robert nodded and slowly they walked down the road together. Robert had lots of time to look in the shop windows.

At last they reached the new hamburger place and went inside. Great Granny sat down at a small round table.

'What would you like?' Robert asked. 'D'you want a cup of tea?'

Great Granny peered at the writing above the serving counter. 'Shall I tell you what I'd *really* like?' she asked.

Robert nodded.

'I'd like one of those bubbly milk shakes with a straw. D'you think I could?'

'Have I got enough money?' Robert asked.

'A pound coin would be just enough for two,' Great Granny said.

Robert smiled. 'Then you can,' he said. 'What flavour?'

'Let me think,' said Great Granny. 'What will you have?'

'Strawberry,' said Robert at once.

'Then may I have chocolate flavour?' asked Great Granny.

Robert went over to the counter and asked the young man who was serving for a chocolate and a strawberry milk shake.

'Right you are,' said the young man, turning on the machine which bubbled up the milk. 'That'll be a pound, please.'

'Thank you,' said Robert handing over his pound coin.

Very carefully, he carried the big cardboard mugs of milk shake back to Great Granny's table. Luckily they had plastic lids on top so that they couldn't spill.

'Aren't they *enormous*?' said Great Granny. 'And aren't they delicious?' she added as she sucked up some of the chocolate bubbles. 'Oh, my goodness. What I've been missing.'

'Haven't you had one before?' Robert asked.

'Never,' Great Granny replied. 'They weren't around when I was little.'

'That's a shame,' said Robert.

'But now I'll be in here all the time, knocking them back, won't I?' said Great Granny.

Robert laughed. 'Would you like a suck of my strawberry one?' he asked.

'Ooh,' said Great Granny. 'This *is* fun,' and she took a great suck at Robert's drink. 'Have some of mine,' she said. 'It's only fair.'

So Great Granny and Robert looked around at the new decorations and enjoyed their milk shakes. After a while Robert said, 'These milk shakes are very big.'

Great Granny nodded. 'I don't think I can finish mine,' she said.

Robert sat up straight to try to make more

room in his stomach. 'Nor can I,' he said sadly.

But the young man who had made the milk shakes heard them and called across, 'Why not put the lids back on and take them home?'

Great Granny called back, 'Thank you. That's an excellent idea. Come along, Robert. Push on those lids again and we'll get back to Mrs Hargreaves.'

Some time later Great Granny and Robert rang at Mrs Hargreaves's door. Robert shouted through her letter-box, 'We've got the stuff in case the bees sting you, Mrs Hargreaves.'

'Come on in,' said Mrs Hargreaves opening her front door. 'I must pay you for the bicarb. But I don't want it for bee stings, I want it for making scones.'

Robert turned to Great Granny, 'Then we'd better have some too,' he said.

'No, don't worry,' said Mrs Hargreaves. 'The scones are for the Easter party on Sunday. So you'll have some then.'

'What Easter party?' Robert asked.

'You'll find out on Sunday,' Great Granny said. 'But in the meantime, we've got some baking to do too. It's Good Friday tomorrow and I expect you know what that means.'

Robert shook his head.

'Then I'll tell you tomorrow,' Great Granny said.

The Girl Upstairs

Great Granny and Mrs Hargreaves had a chat while Robert looked at Mrs Hargreaves's ornaments and photographs. She had five green china elephants on her mantelpiece. The biggest one was about the size of Robert's hand, but the smallest one was smaller than his thumb. He liked them very much.

At last Great Granny stood up and said, 'Come along, Robert. We must go and make our lunch. What do you say to Mrs Hargreaves?'

'Thank you for having me,' Robert said.

'And thank *you*, Robert dear,' said Mrs Hargreaves. 'It was very kind of you to do my shopping.'

As Great Granny went across the landing to her front door she called out 'Hullo, Arianna. Hullo, Clio,' to a woman coming up the stairs with a young girl. 'Why don't you use the lift?'

'The exercise does me good,' said Arianna. The little girl looked at Robert and said nothing.

And Robert looked at the girl and said nothing either. Until, that is, he was inside Great Granny's flat with the door shut behind him and then he said, 'That was the lady with the funny voice on the Underground.'

'No, really?' said Great Granny very surprised. 'What a coincidence. They are a Greek family – very pleasant they are – and they live just up the stairs. Arianna, the mother, is having another baby soon and little Clio has just started school last term. I could telephone Arianna and see if she would let Clio come down here to play this afternoon. Would you like that?'

'No,' said Robert. 'No, thank you,' he added.

Great Granny was looking in her kitchen cupboard. 'I was going to do us potatoes in their jackets for lunch,' she said. 'But we've run short of time. How about bacon and eggs?'

'Yes, please,' said Robert.

'And perhaps we could go to the swings over in the park this afternoon,' Great Granny went on.

Then Robert remembered what his mother had said. 'You must have a rest in the afternoon,' he said.

'Oh, bother,' said Great Granny.

'Susan doesn't like having to rest either,' said Robert.

'Your sister and I have a lot in common,' said Great Granny. 'Still, you're quite right. I must be good.'

Robert went over and put his arms round Great Granny's middle. 'Is it a rest if you sit and look at Bagpuss on television?' he asked.

'That would be cheating, I'm afraid,' Great Granny said. 'I have to lie down with my legs up. Doctor's orders.'

'Then I'll tell you what happens,' Robert promised.

So, that afternoon, Robert watched Bagpuss and Great Granny lay on her bed. But no sooner had the programme finished than there was a ring at the front door bell.

'I'm just coming,' Great Granny called.

'It's me, Arianna,' called back the visitor.

'And what can we do for you?' Great Granny asked as she opened the door.

Clio was standing beside her mother. 'We wondered if Robert would like to come to the swings with us,' Arianna said. 'We have met already on the Underground.'

'Yes, Robert told me,' Great Granny said. 'We were thinking of going to the swings too. Shall we all go together this time? But wait. Even better. Why doesn't Clio come with us and let you have a rest? I've just had one and I feel twice the woman.'

Arianna looked at Clio and Clio nodded happily. 'Then that's very kind of you. I would like to put my feet up,' Arianna said.

'Excellent,' said Great Granny. 'Come on in, Clio dear. Robert and I must get our coats on.'

Robert found his coat and Clio watched him put it on. Robert went into the bedroom while Great Granny put on her coat and Clio followed him. Robert went into the bathroom and shut the door behind him. He waited there until he heard Great Granny call, 'Time to go, Robert.' Then he came out and found Clio standing by the front door – still looking at him.

Robert frowned.

'Come along,' said Great Granny. 'Who can open the front door?'

Clio did and then ran over to press the button to make the lift come. She also did all the button-pressing when they were in the lift. Robert leant against the lift wall.

Together they walked down the road to the zebra crossing. Again Clio pressed the button to stop the traffic.

'Hold on to my sticks, both of you,' said Great Granny as they went carefully across the busy road. 'That's the way.'

When they reached the park gates Great Granny said, 'You can run ahead to the swings now if you like.'

Robert looked at Clio to see if she would start running. Clio looked at Robert. Then Robert turned around and started to walk backwards, keeping a little in front of Great Granny. Clio smiled and did the same. Robert turned around and began to walk normally again. Clio did so too. Robert hopped a couple of times. Clio did the same. Robert jumped along with his legs apart. Clio laughed and did likewise.

'I'm Superman,' Robert shouted and spread his arms.

'I'm Super Ted,' Clio whispered and stretched her arms too.

'And I'm Super Great Gran,' shouted Great

Granny waving her sticks in the air. But the children **didn't** hear her. They were running hard towards **the swings**.

Robert **stopped** at the first swing but Clio kept

running. Robert watched her. Suddenly she stopped beside the see-saw and looked back at Robert. Robert nodded and ran on towards her. Clio climbed on to one end of the see-saw and held it level. Robert climbed on to the other end. Clio jumped and Robert pushed down. As Clio landed Robert sailed up. Clio did an extra jump as she landed and Robert came down with a thud. So he did a jump and she thudded down next. Up and down they went until Great Granny arrived, when Clio stood still to stop the see-saw and then ran off to play on the slide.

Great Granny sat down on a park bench and watched Clio and Robert run from the slide to the swings and on to a climbing frame with tyres hanging in the middle. Then they went back to the see-saw again. They played and ran and played and ran.

Suddenly Great Granny called 'Come on, you two, it's raining.' She stood up and began her slow walk to the park gates. This time Robert did what Clio did – or tried to. She hopped, then skipped, then monkey-walked on her hands and feet. Robert looked at his dirty hands after he'd done that and wiped them on his duffle coat. Great Granny and Clio looked at him. 'Not a good idea,' said Great Granny.

Later, when Clio had gone on up the stairs to

her own flat, Robert said, 'She doesn't talk much, does she?'

Great Granny said, 'No, she doesn't. She talks with her eyes instead, I always think. And when you're as deaf as I'm getting that's no bad thing.'

That evening, before he had his bath, the telephone rang.

'It'll be your mother,' Great Granny said as she picked up the receiver. 'Yes, it is,' she said and handed the receiver to Robert.

'Hullo, Mummy,' Robert said. 'Yes, I'm being good. I've been shopping and there's a see-saw where the swings are. I'm having baked beans for supper *again*.' Then he listened to his mother for a while. 'Yes, she had a rest – didn't you, Great Granny? And so did the lady upstairs. She's the one on the Underground with the funny voice. She's got a girl. She talks with her eyes. Well, that's what Great Granny says she does. Yes. Good night.' And he handed the receiver over to Great Granny.

Then, while Great Granny told his mother that she'd had a good rest and wasn't a bit tired, Robert went into the bathroom to make faces at himself in the mirror. But he couldn't make himself talk with his eyes. He couldn't even wink.

The Holiday Railway

That evening Robert pulled a story book out of his suitcase and took it to Great Granny in the kitchen.

'I've got these stories if you can't think of any,' he said.

Great Granny peered at the book. 'Are the words printed large?' she asked.

Robert shook his head. 'A train story would be better really,' he said. 'Then you won't even need glasses.'

'Well,' said Great Granny, 'let's sit down on the settee and I'll try to remember.'

Robert ran and pushed the book back in his suitcase and then helped Great Granny to sit down, propping her sticks against the arm of the settee. He sat down beside her and waited.

'Are you sitting comfortably?' Great Granny asked. 'Then I'll begin.'

'About trains?' asked Robert.

'Oh yes,' Great Granny agreed. 'You see, we

went everywhere on trains when I was little. There weren't many cars and we didn't have one anyway. I always walked to school when I was little. But, once a year, we used to go on a really long train journey. We used to go on holiday to the West Country and we looked forward to it so much we didn't sleep the night before. We were so excited.'

'I didn't sleep much before I came here,' said Robert.

'No. Packing up and going away is far too exciting,' Great Granny agreed. 'And my mother didn't sleep much either. She was so busy packing our holiday trunk with fishing nets and sun hats, sandals and bathers – that's what we called our swimming things. My big brother George took a long fishing rod and my little brother Geoffrey had to take his pillow – he couldn't sleep without it.'

Robert nodded. 'What did you take?' he asked.

'Well,' said Great Granny, trying to remember. 'I know that one year I wanted to take Johnny Jones our donkey – but I wasn't allowed to. So, yes, I remember, I put one of George's white mice inside my coat and took that instead.'

'Good,' said Robert.

'We caught a lovely green and gold, steaming, hissing train in London and shared a carriage with a very kind old gentleman wearing a cape –

that's a coat with slits for your arms to go
through –'

Robert nodded. 'Susan's got one,' he said.

'Yes, of course she has,' said Great Granny.
'And he did conjuring tricks to keep us children
happy. He pulled off our noses and popped them
on again. He let us blow on his pocket watch to
make it open and he conjured pennies out of
Geoffrey's ears.'

'Did Geoffrey like that?' Robert asked.

'Well, no, not much, but it kept the rest of us
interested until it was time for our picnic lunch.
Then we all got very tired of being in the train
and I'm afraid George and I began to kick each
other and stopped being pleased about going on
holiday until, suddenly, our father said "Six-
pence for the first one to see the sea." Then we
looked and looked and forgot to be cross.'

'Did you see the sea first?' Robert asked.

'Of course,' said Great Granny proudly. 'And
we tried to make Geoffrey look but he wouldn't.
You know what little children are. But soon the
train was running along right beside the sea, and
the kind old gentleman said, "We'll be lucky if
we don't get our feet wet."

'"*What?*" said my mother, and at that moment there was a great splash on the side of the
carriage and the sea shot in. So we had to put our
feet up on the seats. Which was very nice, be-

cause we were always being told not to put our feet on chairs and covers. The old gentleman said, "It often happens when the tide's up and there's a wind blowing. Remember to wear your boots next time."'

'Did Geoffrey get wet?' Robert asked.

'Not then, because he was sitting on Mother's lap,' Great Granny explained. 'But later – oh dear me. You see, our train stopped at a station which was right beside the beach. We all got out and Father ran to the guard's van to get our luggage. Mother said goodbye and thank you to the old gentleman and then, at last, Geoffrey turned round and *saw the sea*. A great smile came over his face and he held up his arms and staggered one, two, three, down the steps on to the beach. Then he ran. He'd only just learnt to *walk* but now he *ran* straight down the beach and into the sea. My mother stepped back from the train and gave a yelp of horror when she spotted Geoffrey.'

'Eeee,' squeaked Robert.

'Yes, like that,' said Great Granny. 'But meanwhile George was racing to the rescue. He had just learnt how to play rugby football at school and it came in very useful. He gave a diving jump into the sea – it's called a "flying tackle" – and grabbed Geoffrey round his fat little middle and they landed – splash – and rolled over in the

waves together. All the train passengers who had
seen the rescue gave a great cheer and George
carried Geoffrey out of the sea and back to my
mother. "Thank you, George," my mother said
quietly and clutched Geoffrey all dripping wet
against her smart white holiday coat. My father
said nothing but walked us all across the road to
the hotel where we were staying. The boys and
Mother stood outside while Father and I went to
ask for some towels for them. And, while Father
was telling the hotel man about George's brave
rescue, I suddenly began to cry and cry.'

'Why?' said Robert looking up at Great
Granny because she suddenly sounded so sad.

'Because I couldn't find George's mouse. I had
looked inside my coat and blouse, and couldn't
find it anywhere. "I've left my mouse on the

train," I cried. "We must go after it." And then my poor Father got cross. "Enough is enough," he said. "You can all stay at home next year."'

'Did you?' Robert asked.

Great Granny shook her head. 'No,' she said. 'We always went back. After all, George was quite a hero. Everyone wanted to see the boy who had rescued his little brother.'

'What happened to the mouse?' Robert asked.

'We never knew for sure,' said Great Granny. 'But George thought it probably climbed into the old gentleman's cape and lived happily ever after in the West Country.'

Later, when Robert was kissing Great Granny good night, he said, 'How did the sea get into the railway carriage?'

Great Granny thought for a moment. 'I've no idea,' she said. 'But I'll tell you what I'll do. I'll write to Geoffrey and ask him. He knows everything about that Great Western Railway, and he can write and tell you all about it.'

Good Friday

Next morning Robert didn't wake up so early. When he opened his eyes he saw that Great Granny was up already. He got out of bed and ran through to the kitchen.

'Good morning,' said Great Granny. 'Did you sleep well?'

'Yes, thank you,' said Robert. 'It's Good Friday.'

'That's right, well done,' said Great Granny.

'You did tell me,' said Robert.

'Oh yes, of course I did. And that means we must make – what?'

'I don't know,' said Robert.

'Then I'll tell you. But come and look at something in the bedroom first.'

Robert followed Great Granny back into the bedroom and she pointed to a cross hanging beside her bed. 'D'you see?' she said. 'The person on the cross is our Lord Jesus. He died like that so that we can go to heaven when we die. It happened on this day nearly two thousand years ago. That's why it's called *Good* Friday.'

'But that was really sad,' said Robert.

'Yes – horribly sad,' Great Granny agreed. 'And his mother and friends – they must have cried and cried. But later of course they had a wonderful surprise.'

'What?' Robert asked.

'I'll tell you on Sunday,' Great Granny said. 'But first we've got to make some things with crosses on them. Can you guess? Hot cross . . .'

'Hot cross buns,' Robert shouted.

'Right first time,' said Great Granny. 'One a penny, two a penny, hot cross buns. If you have no daughters, give them to your sons – or great-grandsons. How about that?'

'Yes, yes,' said Robert happily. 'When can we do them?'

'This morning, while I can still think straight,' said Great Granny. 'And I just thought we might ask Arianna and Clio to tea to help us eat them.'

Robert nodded. 'I can make us our breakfasts – but not porridge,' he said.

'Lovely,' said Great Granny. 'That is a treat. I like brown bread and butter, please. I'll just get out my cookery book and find the recipe for hot cross buns.'

After breakfast Robert brushed his teeth and got dressed. Great Granny combed his hair –

front and back because he'd forgotten all about it
– and tidied up the sitting room and made her
bed. Robert had to make his own because Great
Granny couldn't bend down that far. He pulled
up the sheets and blankets using Great Granny's
criss-cross gadget which helped her to pick up
things without bending. And he put his new
pyjamas beside Panda and covered them both up
with his old eiderdown Horror.

In the meanwhile Great Granny was busy in
the kitchen. Robert could hear her talking to
herself. 'Flour and currants. Spice. Now where's

that baking tin gone? Sugar. Yeast in the fridge.
What else? Of course. A bit of butter. I'll be
forgetting my own name next.'

'It's Rosie,' Robert shouted from the bed
room.

'So it is, thank you. Come along quickly. I
need help,' Great Granny called back.

Robert ran through to the kitchen. 'Can you
wash your hands and then crumble the yeast into
that saucepan of milk? Then I rely on you to tell
me when all the yeast has popped up to the top of
the milk again,' said Great Granny.

Robert dried his hands on the kitchen towel
and unwrapped the lump of yeast. 'It smells,' he
said.

'Nice or nasty?' Great Granny asked.

Robert began to crumble it into the saucepan
of milk.

'I think nasty – a bit,' he said.

'I think so too – a bit,' said Great Granny. 'But
it's wonderful stuff. It makes the buns grow.
Like magic, really.'

'Here it comes,' Robert shouted as a little piece
of yeast bobbed up to the top of the milk and
began to bubble. 'Now there's lots jumping up.
It *is* magic.'

'Good. While I mix up the bun mixture I want
you to mix some flour and water to make the
crosses.'

And Great Granny found a spare mixing bowl
and poured in some flour. Then she added some
cold water. 'Now, use your fingers and make
that into a paste.'

Robert paddled his fingers in the flour. Then
he put in his whole hand and stirred it round. The
flour and water turned into a sticky mess. He
used both hands and squeezed the sticky mess,
trying to make it into a ball. Great Granny
hummed, 'One a penny, two a penny, hot cross
buns.' Robert sighed.

'Having trouble?' said Great Granny.

'No – yes,' said Robert. 'I'm not very good at
this. We made bread at play group and Mrs May
said "Oh dear" at my bit.'

'Oh dear indeed,' said Great Granny. 'Yes, you are getting in a mess. The trouble is, so am I. It's rather a long time since I've made hot cross buns.' And she sighed too.

'I want to blow my nose,' Robert said. 'But my hands are all covered in this stuff.'

'Then I'm sorry to say it, but you'll just have to sniff,' said Great Granny. 'Soldier on, my love. That paste will get drier as you handle it.'

And it did. Robert was able to pull off little bits and make them into flat sausages.

'That's the way,' said Great Granny.

'It's working,' said Robert in surprise.

'So's mine,' said Great Granny cheerfully, throwing a handful of currants into her bowl. She pushed a few currants towards Robert. 'Cooks' perks,' she said.

'Like the mince pies at Christmas,' said Robert, remembering.

'I think this dough ought to make more than twelve buns,' said Great Granny. 'Why don't we ask Mrs Hargreaves to tea too?'

'Yes,' said Robert.

He watched Great Granny pull off small pieces of dough, make them into balls and flatten them on to the baking tin. Then he put two sausages of paste on each bun to make a cross. Great Granny covered the tin with a cloth and put the buns on the warm stove.

'We'll look at them in half an hour. They should have grown – if we're lucky,' she said.

And they *did*. Half an hour later Great Granny took off the cloth and each bun was nearly twice as big. Some of the crosses had slid off sideways. 'Never mind,' said Great Granny. 'And now I want you to brush each bun with sugar water, Robert. Then they'll be sticky and shiny when they're baked.'

Soon the flat was filled with the lovely smell of baking buns. Mrs Hargreaves looked in because the smell was so good, and Robert asked her to tea. Clio and Arianna arrived just as the buns were ready to come out of the oven, and when Clio saw them her eyes shone as much as the shiny brown buns.

'You can have one at tea-time,' Robert told her.

And Clio nodded very hard indeed.

Great Granny's Bad Idea

After all the friends had been to tea, after he got undressed and after his bath, Robert said, 'Can I have another story tonight – please? About when you were bad.'

'Good, you mean,' said Great Granny. 'I was *never* bad.'

'Oh yes, you were,' Robert shouted.

'Rubbish,' said Great Granny. 'You must be thinking of somebody else.'

'No, you,' said Robert. 'Tell me about the time the bees stung you. That sounds good.'

'It was not at all good, young man,' said Great Granny. 'But if you stop hopping about and sit down I'll see what I can remember.'

Great Granny eased herself down on to the settee and Robert sat down beside her, leaning against her arm.

'Well,' Great Granny began. 'It all happened when I was very small. Smaller than you, probably. My mother was having a tea party in the garden. It was a lovely sunny afternoon, but I think I must have been the only child there, because I had nothing to do. The grown-ups talked and talked. You know how grown-ups do.'

Robert nodded.

'And I sat and looked at the flowers in the flower bed in front of the tea table. They were lovely. Snapdragons they were. The sort you can squeeze the sides of and they pop open – snap – like dragons' mouths. Lovely. Well, I picked a couple and was busy making them snap when – suddenly – I saw a bee land on a flower just beside me. It was *fascinating*. I watched it and watched it. It went head first into the flower until it disappeared. Then it backed out all covered in powdery pollen and buzzed off to the next flower.

'I watched and watched. Then I had a bad idea.'

Robert shook his head and looked at Great Granny.

'Well, I was *very* young – not a wise old rising-five like you,' said Great Granny. 'So I decided to play a trick on that bee. Oh dear. I cupped my hands over the flower it had just gone into. What a surprise I thought it would get when it backed out and found itself in the dark inside my hand. And it *did* get a surprise – and so

did I. It went *s-s-s-sting* straight into the palm of my little hot hand. Here, d'you see, on the fat part where my thumb joins on.'

Robert looked at Great Granny's hand but he couldn't see a mark. 'It must have gone,' Great Granny explained. 'But, my goodness, it *did* hurt. I yelled and yelled and one lady spilt her tea down her smart dress because I gave her such a shock. But my kind mother picked me up and ran into the kitchen with me and several ladies followed. I'm afraid I made an awful fuss. And then somebody said "Bicarbonate of soda – that's the stuff for bee stings." I can remember my mother looking in the jam cupboard and getting out a little white drum – very like the one you bought for Mrs Hargreaves. She put a bit on a tea saucer and mixed it into a paste with a drop of water.'

'Like I did for the hot cross buns,' said Robert.

'Well, I don't think she made quite such a mess.' Great Granny said. 'Then she spread some on to my hand. There was a little hole to show where the bee had stung me. I stopped crying then and one lady said I was very brave.'

'Then what did you do?' Robert asked.

'I went into the front garden and waited for my brother George to come home from school, so that I could show him my sting.'

'What did he say?'

'He said "Is that all? I've been stung millions of times." But I didn't believe him.'

'No, I don't either,' said Robert. 'Because I'm nearly five and I've *never* been stung. But I think I'll get some soda stuff.'

'A good idea,' Great Granny agreed. 'And if you still don't get stung you can always use it for making scones, can't you?'

Seeing the Sights

Robert and Great Granny were doing the washing-up on Easter Saturday morning when there was a ring at the front door bell.

It was Clio and her father. Robert hadn't seen him before. He had a black moustache and the same twinkling dark eyes that Clio had.

'Good morning, Kyri,' said Great Granny. 'You're up early for a Saturday morning.'

'Far too early,' said Clio's father. 'I've promised Clio a trip on one of the sight-seeing buses, you see. And she thought Robert might come along. What d'you think?'

Robert glowed. 'Oh yes, yes,' he said.

Great Granny smiled. 'What a wonderful idea,' she said. 'It seemed such a pity to come to London and not see the sights. But I didn't see how I could manage it. You're an angel, Kyri.'

'Do angels have moustaches?' Kyri asked Robert. But Robert didn't know, so he ran off to dress as fast as he could.

Great Granny combed his hair and said, 'Then I'll see you home for a late lunch, Robert. Be good. Hold on to Kyri's hand, and have a lovely time.'

Clio, Kyri and Robert walked along to the Underground station and caught the train that went to Victoria Station – right in the middle of London. Robert recognised the station. It was the one he had come to with his mother.

Outside the station there were lots of red double-decker buses.

'Now, we must find the right bus,' said Kyri. 'One to take us round all the best sights.'

'I want to see where the Queen lives, please,' Robert said.

'I think I can fix that,' said Kyri. 'Ah, this is the bus we want. Let's go upstairs so that we can see everything.'

The children climbed up the steep stairs and Kyri climbed behind them to catch them if they slipped. But they didn't. Clio caught Robert's hand, walked quickly down to the front of the bus and sat down in the front seat. She had thought a lot about this treat and knew where she wanted to sit. Robert sat beside her and Kyri sat behind them.

Soon the bus was full of other passengers talking and making a great noise.

'I can't tell what they're saying,' Robert said.

'That's because they're foreigners, like me,' said Kyri. 'But they are talking their own languages.'

'Can you talk like that?' Robert asked Clio.

Clio nodded and smiled hard.

'That's clever,' said Robert.

Suddenly the bus began to shiver and shake. 'We're off,' said Kyri. Clio pretended to hold a huge steering wheel in front of her. So Robert pretended to push forward a gear handle and pressed with his feet on some pretend pedals. Slowly the bus moved forward and turned into the busy traffic. Kyri pointed to a clock standing on an island in the road.

'There's Little Ben,' he said. 'We'll see Big Ben later.'

The bus swayed on along the road and Robert looked down at all the cars and taxis far below him. 'We're the kings of the castle,' he said. 'And they're the dirty rascals.'

'Soon we'll see the Queen's castle – well, palace really,' said Kyri. 'Look as we turn the corner. There's Buckingham Palace. And d'you see the guards outside?'

Clio and Robert looked and looked. 'She hasn't got any trees,' Clio whispered.

'There are hundreds round the back,' Kyri whispered back.

The bus went past the palace and on down a

wide road with lots of trees.

'Tell me when you see Big Ben,' Kyri said.

Suddenly Robert shouted, 'There it is,' and fell over, bump, because the bus had stopped at some traffic lights. A lady in a seat near him picked him up and began to brush the dirt off his trousers. 'Thank you very much,' Kyri said to her. 'You'd be safer sitting down, Robert,' he said. Clio giggled and Robert sat down crossly.

'But that was very clever of you to spot Big Ben,' Kyri went on. 'I like the new gold paint. It's been cleaned – had its dirt brushed off.'

'Like you,' Clio whispered to Robert.

'I saw it on Blue Peter,' Robert said.

'Now, we'll soon be coming to Trafalgar Square,' Kyri said, 'and you'll see Nelson's

Column. D'you know who Nelson was?'

Robert and Clio shook their heads.

'He was a great sailor,' Kyri said. 'But he only had one arm and one eye.'

The children looked hard, watching out for Nelson's Column.

'Fountains! Look fountains!' Robert shouted suddenly, standing up again. And all the passengers on the bus looked to where he was pointing. He could see two lovely fountains spraying water high into the air – higher even than the top of the bus. Robert looked excitedly at Clio. But she was gazing up and smiling broadly. She was looking at Nelson on top of his column. 'He's got *two* legs,' she said happily.

'Not to mention four stone lions and thousands of pigeons,' said Kyri.

Some time later the bus arrived back at Victoria Station. The children and Kyri waited until everybody else had got off the bus before climbing down the stairs themselves. Robert was very sorry to get off the bus. 'That was really good,' he said to Kyri.

'Next time,' said Kyri, 'we'll get along to see the Tower of London, shall we?'

Robert looked up at Kyri and nodded and stopped dead.

'Look,' he said pointing up over Kyri's shoulder. Clio and Kyri turned to look where he was

pointing. 'That's Concorde,' Robert said.

'I think you're right. Yes,' said Kyri, 'I'm sure it is. What a beautiful plane it is.'

'I can tell James about it. I've seen Concorde. I can tell Richard and Rosie and Mum and Great Granny,' Robert went on.

They stood and watched the huge aeroplane until it disappeared behind a building. Then they went down the steps to catch the Underground train home to Great Granny.

When they arrived outside Great Granny's flat there was a lovely smell of frying onions. Kyri rang the bell. Great Granny opened the door and Robert ran in to hug her.

'I saw Concorde,' he said. 'I did.'

'Oh, how wonderful,' said Great Granny. 'I saw it once over the park there. And I *was* excited. What a lucky boy you are. Thank you, Clio, and thank you Kyri. And don't forget about tomorrow, will you?'

Kyri said 'No, we won't forget. Goodbye, Robert.'

'Goodbye,' said Robert. 'Thank you for taking me.'

'Thank you for coming, Robert,' said Kyri bowing grandly.

But Clio wrinkled her nose at Robert and ran off up the stairs.

'That was really good,' Robert said to Great Granny as she shut the front door.

'And fancy seeing Concorde,' Great Granny said.

Robert sighed. 'Yes,' he said. 'That was really best of all. Now I've seen Concorde.'

And, that afternoon, while Great Granny had her rest, Robert drew pictures of Concorde to show his friends when he got home.

Easter Day

Early next morning Robert woke up and whispered, 'It's Easter Sunday.'

Great Granny moved her head and looked down at him.

'Awake already?' she said.

'Yes,' Robert replied. 'What happened on Easter Sunday? You said you'd tell me.'

'Well,' said Great Granny slowly. 'D'you remember how sad – how *heart-broken* the friends of Jesus were when he died on Good Friday? Yes. I expect they just cried miserably all Saturday. But on Sunday morning, while it was still dark, they went to the tomb where they had put his poor body and – the most amazing thing –'

'What?' Robert asked.

'He wasn't there. Gone. They couldn't believe their eyes. But two young men – angels they were –'

'Like Kyri?' asked Robert.

'Yes – I bet they looked *just* like Kyri,' Great

Granny agreed. 'Well, they said, "He isn't here. You must go and look for him." And Jesus's friends went back home to look for him. But one friend, Mary, saw a gardener and asked him And d'you know, he *was* Jesus. He wasn't a gardener at all. She was so pleased I expect she started crying all over again, don't you?'

Robert nodded.

'So Jesus was alive again and he visited all his old friends and it was such a happy day that we've had Easter Sundays ever since to celebrate. And that's why we're having an Easter party at lunch-time.'

Robert hopped out of bed – very pleased to think of a party. He went to the window, pulled back the curtain and let out a great shout. 'It's snowed,' he yelled. 'All over. It's all snow.'

'Great heavens, whatever next?' said Great Granny. 'Snow at Easter. What weather!'

'It didn't snow at Christmas,' said Robert excitedly.

'No, it didn't. So I suppose snow at Easter is only fair. Oh dear,' said Great Granny.

'Don't you like snow?' Robert asked, very surprised.

'Well, the trouble is,' Great Granny explained, 'it's so difficult to walk on. I'm frightened of falling over. Just think what a crash I'd make.'

'I'll hold you,' said Robert.

'Thank you,' said Great Granny. 'I dare say we'll cope. Now, I must get up and put on my Easter bonnet.'

So Great Granny slowly got dressed and Robert put out the breakfast plates and his dragon mug.

'Find two eggcups,' Great Granny called. 'We must have eggs on Easter Day, and I'll put some cochineal in the water to colour them pink.'

After breakfast Robert dressed himself and stood by Great Granny's window where he could see down into the street. He was watching

out for a friend of Great Granny's who was giving them a lift to church. 'Here's a white car,' he called. 'It's stopped outside.'

'That'll be Mr Jenkins,' Great Granny said. 'Get on your duffle coat and we'll be off.'

Robert and Great Granny went down in the lift together and out on to the snowy pavement. A man got out of the white car and came towards them. 'What a wonderful hat,' he said. 'A real Easter bonnet.'

'Thank you,' said Great Granny happily. 'Mr Jenkins, this is my great-grandson Robert, who is staying with me.'

Mr Jenkins put out his hand to Robert and Robert shook hands with him. Just like a grown-up. *And* Robert remembered what grown-ups say. 'How do you do,' he said. Well, Great Granny and Mr Jenkins were surprised. So was Robert, because he had never said that before. And Mr Jenkins said 'I'm delighted to meet you, Robert. What d'you think of all this snow?'

'It's very nice,' said Robert politely.

'What rubbish,' said Great Granny, not at all politely. 'It's terrible stuff. I hate it.'

'But I'm sure you loved it when you were seven or eight,' said Mr Jenkins, helping Great Granny into the car. Robert *was* pleased. Nobody had ever thought he was seven or eight before. He sat very upright in the back of the car so that Mr Jenkins would think how tall he was.

The church was full of daffodils and everybody was wishing everybody else a happy Easter. And everybody admired Great Granny's special Easter hat.

When they came out of church the sun was shining and everywhere was dripping.

'It's melting. It's going away,' Robert said, looking at the water running off the church roof.

'So it is,' said Great Granny.

'I won't be able to make a snowman,' Robert said and suddenly felt a thump in the middle of his back.

'And it's not much good for snowballs either,'

said Mr Jenkins rubbing snow off his hands and laughing.

'Are you throwing snowballs at my great-grandson, Mr Jenkins?' said Great Granny. And she scooped some snow off a wall and threw it at Mr Jenkins. But he dodged and the snow hit the priest who was just wishing Robert a happy Easter.

'Oh, I *am* sorry,' Great Granny called. 'I meant to hit Mr Jenkins.'

'That is no excuse,' said the priest. 'What shall we do with her, Robert?' he asked.

'The water's falling on your hat, Great Granny,' Robert shouted. And so it was. The poor Easter bonnet was getting quite soaked by the drips.

'Oh well,' said Great Granny feeling her wet hat. 'My mother always said we shouldn't throw snowballs. And now I know she was right.'

The Easter Party

When Robert and Great Granny got back to the flat they saw that Mrs Hargreaves's front door was open.

'Happy Easter,' Great Granny called and Mrs Hargreaves appeared at her door.

'Hullo,' she said. 'What a shame – that lovely Easter hat. Will it be all right when it dries?'

'It had better be,' Great Granny said. 'Or Robert will have to make me another one. Now, it must be nearly party-time. Where is everybody?'

Just then Robert saw Arianna coming down the stairs.

'I've got the chicken and rice,' she said. 'A happy Easter, everyone. Shall I put it on the table?'

'That's right,' said Great Granny. 'And what are the others bringing?'

'I think the Dixons are bringing some salads and the Williamses are bringing some wine and fruit juice,' Arianna said.

'Those are the families in the flats below,' Great Granny explained to Robert.

'What are we having for pudding?' Robert asked. He liked puddings.

'Wait and see,' said Great Granny.

Soon the flat was full of people carrying dishes and knives and forks and glasses and saying 'Hullo' to Robert. And some of them gave him an Easter egg. So that by the time everybody had arrived for the party Robert had no less than six Easter eggs. He went and put them in a row on his bed and Clio came to look at them. She looked and looked at them and Robert said, 'D'you like white chocolate?'

Clio nodded hard.

'I don't. You have it,' said Robert. And he picked up the egg which was made of white chocolate and gave it to her.

Clio opened the packet and began to eat the white chocolate egg – just like that. So Robert opened up the one with Smarties in it and began to eat that. Clio laughed and put out her hand for some Smarties and Robert gave her some.

'I like chocolate,' said Robert with his mouth full of it. Clio nodded and poured all the Smarties into her mouth in one go. Robert laughed and began to open *another* Easter egg.

Well, luckily that egg was hollow – it had

nothing inside – and Robert ate one half and Clio began to eat the other. Then Robert noticed that Clio wasn't laughing any more. She wasn't even smiling. She felt sick.

And as Robert looked at her he began to feel sick too. He picked up the three eggs he had left and put them on Great Granny's bed. Clio watched him do it and nodded.

Just then Mrs Hargreaves looked into the bedroom. 'Lunch-time, dears,' she said. 'I've got my daughter Clare's little table for you in the corner of the kitchen. Everyone else will have to sit on the floor, by the looks of it.'

Robert and Clio walked through all the

grown-ups to Great Granny's kitchen and saw a little table with two plates with chicken salad on them, two glasses of Coca-Cola and two beautiful chocolate Easter eggs with yellow ribbon tied round them.

'No thank you,' said Robert to Mrs Hargreaves. Clio just shook her head.

Mrs Hargreaves looked at them for a moment before she said, 'That's chocolate round your mouth, isn't it?' Robert nodded and felt he was going to cry. 'Sorry,' he said.

Then Mrs Hargreaves did a very kind thing. 'Look,' she said, 'we won't spoil your Great

Granny's party by telling her that you've been guzzling those eggs. You two go quietly and lie down in the bedroom until you feel better. I'll clear your lunch away.'

'Thank you,' said Robert and went back to lie down on one end of his bed while Clio lay down at the other end. They didn't look at the three eggs on Great Granny's bed. Not at all. But while they lay very still they didn't feel so horrid. And soon they were both sound asleep.

Some time later, when all the flat people had cleared up and gone away after the party, Great Granny and Arianna came into the bedroom.

Robert opened one eye and quickly closed it again.

'Here are the Sleeping Beauties,' Great Granny said. 'Tired out after their Easter party. I seem to remember being just as tired after an Easter party myself when I was little. My godmother gave us an egg hunt in her garden, you see. My brother George found *dozens*. I didn't, but he let me help him to eat them. Lots and lots of lovely eggs. We ate and ate and then I looked at him and he looked at me and – oh dear . . .'

Clio snorted.

'What's that?' said Great Granny.

Robert began to laugh.

'Oh, you're awake are you?' said Great Granny. 'How about a lovely piece of Easter egg? Oh. Don't you want any? Are these ones on my bed for me? How very kind. I shall enjoy those. But perhaps I'd better not eat them all at once.'

'No,' said Robert. 'They aren't nice all at once.'

'Very wise,' Great Granny agreed. 'It would never do to feel sick, would it, Clio?' And she winked at Clio who laughed and stood up and gave Great Granny a goodbye hug.

'I think a quiet evening watching television would suit us tonight,' said Great Granny. 'We must be very well and strong for tomorrow,' she added.

'Why?' Robert asked.

'Because I've been on the telephone to your mother and father. And tomorrow they're coming to fetch you home.'

Flying Bells

When Robert was tucked up in bed that night Great Granny propped herself against her high bed and said 'Have I ever told you about the flying bells?'

'No. Tell me now,' said Robert, very pleased not to go to sleep just yet.

'Well,' said Great Granny. 'I was a very lucky little girl, now I come to think of it, because I had a French godmother. She used to visit us quite a lot and I loved her very much. Then, one year, she said to my mother and father "Why not bring the family and spend Easter in France?"

'Just think of that – Easter in France. We were excited. Of course it meant more train journeys *and* a trip across the sea as well.'

'You were lucky,' said Robert.

'Wasn't I just?' Great Granny agreed. 'And when our train reached the town in France where my godmother lived, there she was standing on the station, ready to take us to her house in a horse and carriage. My father walked with Geoffrey because the carriage was rather full and Geoffrey was feeling sick with all that travelling.'

Robert nodded. 'Susan's sick sometimes,' he said.

'She'll grow out of it,' Great Granny said. 'Anyway, as soon as we arrived at my god-mother's house she took us straight up to the attic at the very top of the house. There were two camp-beds for George and me and lots of in-teresting junk. Old paintings in gold frames. Tables with a leg missing. Trunks which might have had treasure inside. All sorts of things. And, best of all, in the corner through a low door was a real tower.'

Robert sighed and Great Granny sighed too. 'Not a very big tower, mind you,' she said. 'But it had steps going up – about six – and a window. My godmother took us up and opened the win-dow. We looked out and saw roofs and chimneys and, far away at the end of the town, the trees of the great forest that stretched for miles. It was a lovely place to be.

'Suddenly, my godmother said, "Can you hear any church bells?" Well, we listened and listened. George nearly fell out of the window trying to hear, but we couldn't. "Well, you won't," said my godmother – much to our

surprise. "You won't hear a church bell in all France. They've flown away to Rome."

'Well, George and I looked at each other. We didn't know church bells *could* fly and we didn't even know where Rome was. But my god-mother said, "Don't worry. On Easter Sunday they'll all be back and when they come they'll drop eggs for all the boys and girls to find in their gardens."

'I was very excited, but George whispered, "Bells can't fly. I think it's just a story." And my godmother heard him. She said, "Just you wait and see, young man, just you wait and see."

'Two days later it was Easter Sunday. George and I woke up at crack of dawn and crept downstairs to let ourselves out into the garden. It was a lovely garden – full of spring flowers and bushes and trees with their branches twined together. And all around it had a very high grey stone wall.

'We ran here and there and peered under the bushes and in the flower pots and even in the rubbish heap. But could we find an egg? We could not. And George got crosser and crosser. "I knew it was just a story. A silly old story," he said and stamped about very naughtily. However, later on we all went off to church together. Suddenly my father pointed to the sky and said, "There's a bell. D'you see?" We all stopped and stared and, at that moment, the church bells began to ring out across the town. "Ding, dang, dong. Ding, dang, dong" – in the way French bells do. And George wanted to run back *at once* to search for eggs. But Mother said they'd still be there when we got back.

'After church was over, my kind godmother let George and me have her house key. And we ran on ahead and let ourselves in. We rushed through the house and out into the garden and there – all over the paths and flower beds – were dozens of little coloured sugar eggs.'

'Not chocolate,' said Robert.

'No, not chocolate, sugar ones. But I soon found that too many sugar eggs can make you feel just as horrid as too many chocolate ones. But you wouldn't know about that, would you?'

Robert laughed and Great Granny winked at him.

'Did you have to lie down?' he asked.

'We did,' said Great Granny, 'nearly all the afternoon in our attic bedroom. We didn't explore those trunks at all. In fact, I fell sound asleep and didn't wake up until I heard the terrible yelling.'

'What terrible yelling?' Robert asked, sitting up in bed.

'That's what I wondered. So I jumped off my bed and ran to the window in the tower because the yelling was coming from outside. I looked out and there was George. He was clinging to the top of the great high wall around the garden, shouting and bellowing because he was stuck and frightened. Suddenly, my father rushed out of the house and, on the other side of the wall, a fat man with a black moustache burst out of the house next door, and they both shouted at George – who couldn't hear anyway – he was making such a din.

'Both my father and the fat man got their garden ladders and climbed up to rescue George. They met at the top of the wall and shook hands politely. And George stopped crying and clung to my father and explained that he'd climbed the wall to see if there were any spare Easter eggs on the other side. Just in case the bells had dropped them in gardens without children, by mistake, you see. My father told the fat man why George had done such a dangerous thing and when the fat man understood what my father was saying he held out his arms to George and said, "Come, my friend,'' in the kindest way. And George's face lit up. All his tears dried up at once and the fat man carried him down the ladder on his side of the wall.

'I ran downstairs then and found my father putting away the ladder in the garden shed. "Where's George gone?" I asked. "Gone to make himself sick on more eggs, I dare say,'' my father said. And, d'you know, even though I'd only just stopped feeling sick from that morning's eggs, I still wanted to go with George.'

'Did George come back?' Robert asked.

'He did,' said Great Granny.

'Stuffed with eggs?' asked Robert.

Great Granny laughed. 'Oh yes,' she said, 'but he had a present for me and Geoffrey from the kind fat man. He brought us a lovely chocolate fish. It really was a beauty. It lay in a white box in blue paper –'

'Like the sea,' said Robert.

'Exactly,' Great Granny agreed. 'And we took it back home with us and didn't eat it at all until my mother's birthday. Then we all had a bit – and it was delicious – but I was sad to see it go, all the same. And now, off to sleep, young man. You mustn't have bags under your eyes in the morning, or your mother will think you've been eating too many eggs. And that would never do, would it?'

The Last Plan

Next morning Robert packed his suitcase and went to look in Great Granny's kitchen cupboards.

'What are you looking for?' Great Granny asked as she put away their breakfast plates.

'I'm looking at things,' Robert explained. 'My mother hasn't got all these things.'

'Well,' said Great Granny. 'Would you like to take anything home?'

'Yes *please*,' Robert said happily and he picked up a packet of brown cubes which Great Granny always put in her gravy.

'Do take those two tins of baked beans,' Great Granny said. 'And there are some of Mrs Hargreaves's good scones left over from the party. I'm sure you and Susan could eat those up. And what about those last few flapjacks?'

So Robert's suitcase was so bulgy with all the good things from Great Granny's cupboards that he had to wait for his father to come and shut it.

Robert's father and mother and sister Susan
arrived just before lunch-time. Robert hugged
them and hugged them – even Susan. And Susan
was so delighted to see him she shouted 'Bert –
Bert,' which she had never said before at all, so
everyone was very pleased. But Robert's father
said *he* would call him 'Bert' too, and then
Robert wasn't so pleased.

For lunch they all ate up the remains of the
chicken salad and some chocolate gateau which
Mr Hargreaves had made. Robert enjoyed it
very much.

'That was delicious,' said Robert's mother
when all the gateau was finished. 'And now we
have a plan,' she went on.

Robert sat up straight. He liked plans. And Great Granny sat up too. 'Oh? What?' she said.

'Well, we thought that perhaps – if you aren't doing anything special in the next week, Granny – whether you might like to come and stay with us. Your room's all ready for you.'

'Oh yes – yes – yes,' Robert shouted, jumping up and running round the table to Great Granny.

Great Granny smiled and smiled. 'Well,' she said, 'Mr Jenkins was going to take me out for a drive on Wednesday, but I could telephone him and explain, couldn't I?'

'Yes – yes,' Robert shouted again.

'And it's Bert's fifth birthday party next week,' Robert's father said. 'You could see he doesn't eat too much party food.'

'As if he would,' said Great Granny, winking at Robert who tried to wink back – but he couldn't.

'Well, that's settled. Lovely,' said Robert's mother. 'Let me help you to pack, Granny.'

Great Granny stood up slowly and happily. 'And this means,' she said, 'that Robert can take *everything* out of the fridge and carry it off with him. You've been longing to do that, haven't you, Robert?'

And Robert laughed and put his hand over one of his eyes and managed to wink hard with the other.

At the End

The day before Robert started school he had a postcard and a letter. The postcard was from Great Granny's brother Geoffrey. It said:

Dear Robert,
I am quite sure that those excellent Great Western Railway carriages would never have let the sea come in. I expect my mother left the window open, don't you? And the sea sloshed in through that.
When your family come to the West Country I'll take you on a real steam train.
With love from your
Great great uncle Geoff

The letter was from Great Granny. It said:

Dear Robert,
Ask your mother or father if they will let you melt half a block of butter in a saucepan.

Stir in three tablespoonsful of sugar, two tablespoonsful of syrup and twenty (count carefully) tablespoonsful of porridge oats, and a pinch of salt.

Then tip the sticky mess into a swiss roll tin (or the lid of a biscuit tin), press it down flat and cook it for about twenty minutes (count carefully again) in a hottish oven.

When you get the tin out of the oven (use oven gloves – not burnt hands) you will find that you've made FLAPJACKS. Cut them into fingers while they're warm and share them with the family when they're cold. *Never* eat them all yourself.

Have an interesting first day at school. I shall telephone you to hear all about it.

And don't forget about our visit to the Zoo.

With all my love,

Great Granny